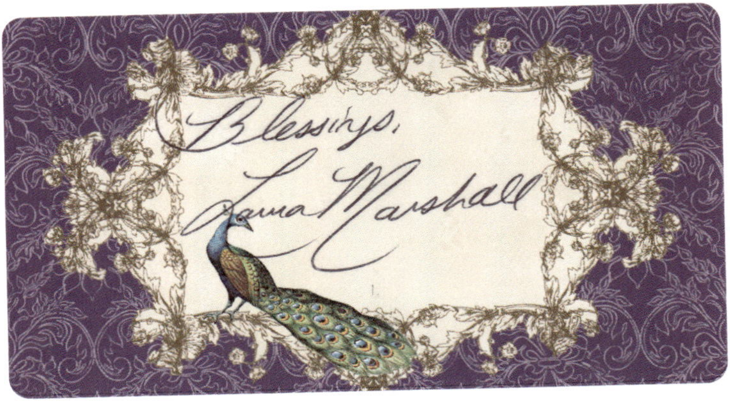
Blessings,
Laura Marshall

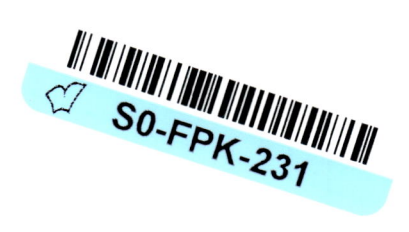

A Mom's Battle Cry for Rest

Laura J. Marshall

Copyright © 2013 Laura J. Marshall

All rights reserved.

"Scripture taken from the New King James Version®. Copyright © 1982 by Thomas Nelson, Inc. Used by permission. All rights reserved."

THE HOLY BIBLE, NEW INTERNATIONAL VERSION®, NIV® Copyright © 1973, 1978, 1984, 2011 by Biblica, Inc.™ Used by permission. All rights reserved worldwide.

ISBN-10: 1481140884
ISBN-13: 978-1481140881

A Mom's Battle Cry for Rest

LAURA J. MARSHALL

DEDICATION

Dedicated to my husband and children with thanks to my supportive extended family and friends. Special thanks to my Pastors Mark and Sylvia Lipscomb at Rock Church in Fredericksburg, Virginia who encourage and equip those in their flock and lead the church to the Good Shepherd.

A Mom's Battle Cry for Rest

LAURA J. MARSHALL

CONTENTS

1 Introduction
2 Day One ~ The Spice Rack
3 Day Two ~ The Cake
4 Day Three ~ The Towel
5 Day Four ~ The Party
6 Day Five ~ The Sword
7 Day Six ~ The Robe
8 Day Seven ~ The Tub
9 In The End
   A Note And Gift from Laura

A MOM'S BATTLE CRY FOR REST

INTRODUCTION

My haggard body rolled out of bed early, packing snacks, lunches, signing papers, and with a swoosh of the yellow school bus tires through the leaf strewn puddle, I am back in bed. A mother of five boys lying in bed during the day? I was up most of the night ill.

Yet, while I "languish" here, I swear I hear voices.

Voices from the kitchen downstairs: the piles of dirty dishes and cereal boxes left out from breakfast yelling to me. I can hear the distant call of pants needing washing from down the hallway. These voices are accompanied by my list-making brain, continually adding to the stacks of to-do's and oh-no's!

In this book, we will explore the application of the Lord's Rest for Moms.

And although this book is about rest, you're going to have to do some work to get there. Preparation. Preparing your heart and changing some of the moments in your days to enter into the rest and refreshment of the Lord.

Is it worth it? Yes.

Is it life-changing? For the better, yes!

So, let's commence shutting those pesky nagging voices out and hear God's voice on the matter. This is A Mom's Battle Cry for Rest.

DAY ONE ~ THE SPICE RACK

Most spices are bitter by themselves. They were not meant to be eaten alone. When they are added to different foods such as meats, they enhance and add depth to the flavor.

Work can be a bitter herb when done without rest. Let's look at the Israelites in Exodus 1:13-14:

"So the Egyptians made the children of Israel serve with rigor. And they made their lives *bitter with hard bondage* - in mortar, in brick, and in all manner of service in the field. All their service in which they made them serve was with rigor."

The bondage of hard labor made the Israelites bitter.

I've been sick for five weeks now. Five weeks of a sore throat, headache, cough, and congestion. My patience is waning.

My time has been broken up with the regular day-to-day things we Moms do, but also with trying to rest. More time has been spent than usual in my chair with a laptop, surfing the web. I've rushed through the usual cleaning, laundry, and dinners to get by.

I.don't.feel.well. I've been miserable, but not just with illness. I am becoming bitter *even* though I've had rest. I'm bitter at the house not being clean, bitter at work, bitter at my children for making constant messes, even bitter at my husband for going to work. I am bitter at myself and even *bitter at rest*.

Bitter at REST itself. I feel the guilt of sitting down. The guilt of sitting…..maybe too much.

The Bible says in Proverbs 24:30-34:

I went by the field of a lazy man,
And by the vineyard of the man devoid of understanding;
And there it was, all overgrown with thorns;
Its surface was covered with nettles;
Its stone wall was broken down.
When I saw it, I considered it well;
I looked on it and received instruction:
A little sleep, a little slumber,
A little folding of the hands to rest;
So shall your poverty come like a prowler,
And your need like an armed man.

This passage had me confused about rest. How can a little folding of the hands be bad? Was I lazy? Had I *become* lazy, feeling justified due to my illness?

Today, I decided to tackle the house. It's December and the house needs cleaning and decorating. I cleaned the first half of the day angry. I disliked everyone in my household as I muttered under my breath and cleaned with one hand clenched.

While cleaning the whole upstairs, the kids' bathroom, behind the TV, organizing the Wii games, and dusting, God showed me how neglectful I had been the past few weeks. I did enough to get by, but where was my "excellence"?

I had grown complacent and feeling justified, I did just barely what I had to, hence the guilt. The Holy Spirit was convicting me. It's okay to be sick and rest, but I had taken advantage.

God doesn't want us to just slide by. He wants our best, in everything: Our best in working around our homes, taking care of our families, and at our workplace. It's not about earning grace, it's about 1 Corinthians 10:31, "So whether you eat or drink or whatever you do, do it all for the glory of God." This is our offering to the Lord.

Bitterness rears its head for all of us in differing areas. I was bitter at myself and also at my workload. I had let things pile up. I also hadn't asked for much help, but was more content to relax with the kids after school and watch TV than have us all pitch in and get things done. How do we root out bitterness?

The first way of getting rid of bitterness is recognizing that it's there. After that, you manually remove the root and put a barrier up so that it doesn't grow back. These are what all of the gardening experts say are the "natural ways" to get rid of an unwanted root.

Manually removing a root is confessing the sin of bitterness and if need be, asking forgiveness from those who we have offended during the course of its growth and life.

I still look around and see all the slush piles that await me. They are never ending: The cleaning, the cooking, dirty dishes, and laundry. No matter how much I do, there is always more…and more…and more. I can get bitter just thinking about it.

How do we know what to tackle, what to leave for another day, which way to turn, and what to do on a daily basis? Prayer and seeking God *first*. It sounds trite, doesn't it? But have you tried it?

When I remember to start my day with prayer, before I get out of bed, God directs my steps. God has instructions even for the minutest details of our lives. I *specifically* ask him to direct each moment, each task, and to lead me to the next. God's plan is always better than our own and He lavishes His love on us in little ways throughout the day. Put your time into His hands.

Isaiah 28:23-29 reads:

Give ear and hear my voice,
Listen and hear my speech.
Does the plowman keep plowing all day to sow?
Does he keep turning his soil and breaking the clods?

When he has leveled its surface,
Does he not sow the black cumin,
And scatter the cumin,
Plan the wheat in rows,
The barley in the appointed place,
And the spelt in its place?
For He instructs him in right judgment,
His God teaches him.
For the black cumin is not threshed with a threshing sledge,
Nor is a cartwheel rolled over the cumin;
But the black cumin is beaten out with a stick,
And the cumin with a rod.
Bread flour must be ground;
Therefore he does not thresh it forever,
Break it with his cartwheel,
Or crush it with his horsemen.
This also comes from the *Lord of hosts,*
Who is wonderful in counsel and excellent in guidance.

It's pretty tedious to hear about how to harvest cumin. I had NO idea that you mustn't use a sledge, whatever that may be, and must beat the black cumin with a stick and another type with a rod. What I gleaned from this passage is that God instructs *and* teaches us in *everything*. Instruction is a methodical approach characterized by ordered and systematic habits or behavior.

How does God instruct us? He instructs us through His Holy Spirit and also by reading His Word. Read with the intention of hearing God speak to you personally. I read the Scriptures and if something pricks me spiritually, I don't move on right away. I let God speak to me through that word. I meditate on it until I feel it personally, sinking into my soul and then into my heart and mind. I take my moments where I can get them. I know from experience that these Scriptures simmer within me throughout the day like something spiced and fragrant http://www.arealchange.com/blog/millionaire-change-world-give-money-live-life-dreamsing in the crockpot and hinting at a delicious meal.

Isaiah 55:10 says:

For as the rain comes down, and the snow from heaven,
And do not return there,
But water the earth,
And make it bring forth and bud,
That it may give seed to the sower
And bread to the eater,
So shall My word be that goes forth from My mouth;
It shall not return to Me void,
But it shall accomplish what I please,
And it shall prosper in the thing for which I sent it.

And so I whisper, *I'm tired.*

He whispers back, *Are you really? How tired are you?*

I shrug, *I'm not really that tired.*

I want to complain…and whine. He listens and nods.

He knows my heart. He knows when I'm being lazy or when I'm truly tired, having handled crying babies, spills, sickness, and everything else in between.

God wants our best. He wants us to seek Him first. Prayer and reading His Word. These are the keys to a life without bitterness. These are the barriers.

The Spice Rack:

Bitterness

Excellence

Prayer

Reading the Word

~

Guide my steps today, dear Lord. In Jesus' name I pray, Amen.

Rest Stop:

Oh, that I had wings like a dove!
I would fly away and be at rest.
Indeed, I would wander far off,
And remain in the wilderness. Selah
I would hasten my escape
From the windy storm and tempest.
Psalm 55:6-8

DAY TWO ~ THE CAKE

God has given me 1,440 minutes today. How am I spending them? Some days I think I did okay with my minutes and then there are days when I'm not so sure. What exactly should I be doing with my days? Am I going to account for each one when I get to heaven?

Let's revisit the story about Martha and Mary found in Luke 10:38-42.

"Now it happened as they went that He entered a certain village; and a certain woman named Martha welcomed Him into her house. And she had a sister called Mary, who also sat at Jesus' feet and heard His word. But Martha was distracted with *much serving*, and she approached Him and said, "Lord, do You not care that my sister has left me to serve alone? Therefore tell her to help me." And Jesus answered and said to her, "Martha, Martha, you are worried and troubled about many things. But one thing is needed, and Mary has chosen that *good part*, which will not be taken away from her."

I've always thought that Martha got the raw deal here. She is *serving* and yet, Mary has chosen the *good part*?

The Bible says, "But God has chosen the foolish things of the world to put to shame the wise, and God has chosen the weak things of the world to put to shame the things which are mighty." (1Cor 1:27)

There is eternal value in *serving*, but the *good part* is "But seek *first* the kingdom of God and His righteousness, and all these things shall be added to you." (Matt 6:33)

"The words that I speak to you are spirit and they are life." (John 6:63)

But Jesus answered him, saying, "It is written, 'Man shall not live by bread alone, but by every word of God." (Luke 4:4)

Jesus' words are life. Jesus is The Cake! Don't miss out on the daily celebration. Mary chose to spend time listening to, learning from, and adoring the Lord. How can we mimic this? Are we laboring to distraction? Are our labors causing us to miss the moments with Jesus?

When I am tired and worried about much, I pause and remember the verses at the end of Matthew 11:25-30. What I sometimes skip are the sentences at the beginning of the passage.

At that time Jesus answered and said, "I thank You, Father, Lord of heaven and earth, that You have hidden these things from the wise and prudent and have revealed them to babes. Even so, Father, for so it seemed good in Your sight. All things have been delivered to Me by My Father, and no one knows the Son except the Father. Nor does anyone know the Father except the Son, and the one to whom the Son wills to reveal Him. Come to Me, all you who labor and are heavy laden, and I will give you rest. Take My yoke upon you and learn from Me, for I am gentle and lowly in heart, and you will find rest for your souls. For My yoke is easy and My burden is light."

Rest is precluded by knowing Jesus. When I stay connected to Jesus, repent of my sins, and read God's Word along the way I will be led by God's Holy Spirit in the *moments* of my days.

How do we get closer to Jesus, learn from Him, adore Him, find His rest? Unconfessed sin can hinder entering into the Lord's Rest.

Psalm 38:3 says:

There is no soundness in my flesh
Because of Your anger,
Nor any *health* in my bones (KJV = Neither is there any *rest* in my bones)
Because of my sin.
For my iniquities have gone over my head;
Like a heavy burden they are too heavy for me.
My wounds are foul and festering
Because of my foolishness.
I am troubled, I am bowed down greatly;
I go mourning all the day long.
For my loins are full of inflammation,

And there is no soundness in my flesh.
I am feeble and severely broken;
I groan because of the turmoil of my heart.

And Psalm 32:

Blessed is he whose transgression is forgiven,
Whose sin is covered.
Blessed is the man to whom the Lord does not impute iniquity,
And in whose spirit there is no deceit.
When I kept silent, my bones grew old
Through my groaning all the day long.
For day and night Your hand was heavy upon me;
My vitality was turned into the drought of summer. Selah
I acknowledged my sin to You,
And my iniquity I have not hidden.
I said, "I will confess my transgressions to the Lord,"
And You forgave the iniquity of my sin. Selah
For this cause everyone who is godly shall pray to You
In a time when You may be found;
Surely in a flood of great waters
They shall not come near him.
You are my hiding place;
You shall preserve me from trouble;
You shall surround me with songs of deliverance. Selah
I will instruct you and teach you in the way you should go;
I will guide you with My eye.
Do not be like the horse or like the mule,
Which have no understanding,
Which must be harnessed with bit and bridle,

Else they will not come near you.
Many sorrows shall be to the wicked;
But he who trusts in the Lord, mercy shall surround him.
Be glad in the Lord and rejoice, you righteous;
And shout for joy, all you upright in heart!

Is there anything I need to go up and set down at the Lord's feet?

"There remains therefore a rest for the people of God. For he who has entered His rest has himself also ceased from his works as God did from His." Hebrews 4:9-10

In Matthew Henry's Concise Commentary on Hebrews 4:1-10, Mr. Henry states, "God has always declared man's rest to be in Him, and His love to be the only real happiness of the soul; and faith in His promises, through His Son, to be the only way of entering that rest."

The Cake:

Knowing Jesus

Repenting of Sin

~

Help me to listen at your feet today, Dear Lord. In Jesus' name I pray, Amen.

Rest Stop:

Repent therefore and be converted, that your sins may be blotted out, so that times of refreshing may come from the presence of the Lord, and that He may send Jesus Christ, who was preached to you before, whom heaven must receive until the times of restoration of all things, which God has spoken by the mouth of all His holy prophets since the world began.
Acts 3:19-21

DAY THREE ~ THE TOWEL

As I pick up a discarded towel off my son's bedroom floor on my way to get my own, I turn around, deciding not to dirty another one. A dirty one is fine for me, right?

I love my family so much. I would give them the last morsel of food and sip of water. So would you. I have an easier time loving them than loving myself. I take my guys to the doctor for their yearly checkups, shots, and when they are sick. Can you or I say that we do the same for ourselves?

Rest is personal, so we're going to make this personal. Not about you loving your children or your spouse, but about loving yourself. You are miraculous. Not for what you do, but for who you *are*. God took the time to really think about you when He created you. He loves you. You are worthy of love. You are worthy of loving yourself. This is one of the hardest lessons.

Ephesians 2:4-10 reads, "But God, who is rich in mercy, *because of His great love with which He loved us*, even when we were dead in trespasses, made us alive together with Christ (by grace you have been saved), and raised us up together, and made us sit together in the heavenly places in Christ Jesus, that in the ages to come He might show the exceeding riches of His grace in His kindness toward us in Christ Jesus. For by grace you have been saved through faith, and that not of yourselves; it is the gift of God, not of works, lest anyone should boast. *For we are His workmanship*, created in Christ Jesus for good works, which God prepared beforehand that we should walk in them."

We are God's workmanship. He loved us so much to create us then He loved us so much that even in our sin, He sent His only Son to die for us. As the Word above says, we were created to walk in the good works God prepared for us beforehand. I believe one of those good works is being kind and loving to ourselves.

Now, don't get me wrong. I have seen how kind and loving some people can be towards themselves. Some people go off the deep end with obsessive dieting, exercise, shopping for clothes, jewelry, et cetera. This is unhealthy as well. Like in all things, moderation is key.

How can you *love yourself* today? There are things we can do daily, weekly, monthly to love ourselves so in the long run we can look down and say, "Hey, I am *loving and taking care of myself* along with my children, husband, and home."

It sounds sensible, doesn't it? Convinced? As a Mom, I've really tried to put this into practice, but when it comes right down to doing certain things for myself, they feel selfish. At least they did. I've had to put it into perspective: Pinpoint, nitty-gritty, dirty towel perspective. How can using a dirty towel be loving myself? It just plain isn't. Would I let one of my children use a dirty towel?

Let's break this down even more. What did you have for lunch today? Yesterday? How long did it take you to eat? I actually timed myself a month or so ago. Not on purpose, but I happened to look at the clock when I started eating and then when I had finished. It took me five minutes. I couldn't believe it. We should be taking the time to care about what we're putting into our bodies and how we're putting it into our bodies.

I have a picture of my youngest son eating lunch when he was four. After preschool, while he played with his toys, I would take the time to prepare a nice lunch on pretty glass plates. I'd call him in and we would sit together with our favorite kid's show on in the background (which just happened to have soothing music and lovely story lines) and talk, laugh, and eat. I loved and enjoyed our lunchtimes together. I still think of them fondly and treasure the memories.

How can I still make those gossamer-laden moments? I can love myself in the little things. I can prepare a nice lunch on a glass plate and read something while I eat that I find enjoyable or watch a show that feeds my soul. Do the gossamer moments have to always be with *someone else*? No, but this is your life. You only get one. If you're hesitant to spend too much time alone with yourself then maybe you're having a hard time loving who you are.

Again it comes down to moderation. To spend *too* much time looking down can force us to lose perspective, heavenly perspective. I try to look up to Christ so I don't see myself too much, but when I do look down, I want to again be able to say, "I *am loving and taking care of myself* along with my children, husband, and home." When I look too closely, I see all my flaws…a nose that looks like somewhere along the way it's been broken or 20 pounds still to lose…a nip here, a tuck there. Would I then be okay enough to love?

It has helped me to remember that we are the temple of the Holy Spirit. 1 Corinthians 6:19-20 says, "Or do you not know that your body is the *temple of the Holy Spirit who is in you*, whom you have from God, and you are not your own? For you were bought at a price; therefore glorify God in your body and in your spirit, which are God's."

And that Christ lives in me. Galatians 2:17-21 says, "But if, while we seek to be justified by Christ, we ourselves also are found sinners, is Christ therefore a minister of sin? Certainly not! For if I build again those things which I destroyed, I make myself a transgressor. For I through the law died to the law that

I might live to God. I have been crucified with Christ; it is no longer I who live, but *Christ lives in me*; and the life which I now live in the flesh I live by faith in the Son of God, who loved me and gave Himself for me. I do not set aside the grace of God; for if righteousness comes through the law, then Christ died in vain."

Another way key way we can love ourselves is by giving ourselves *the gift of rest*.

Love God, love your family, love yourself.

The Towel:

Love

~

Dear Jesus, Help me to be loving and kind to myself in little ways throughout the day. In Jesus' name I pray, Amen.

Rest Stop:

Return to your rest, my soul, for the Lord has been good to you.
Psalm 116:7

_____
_____
_____
_____
_____
_____
_____
_____
_____
_____
_____
_____
_____
_____
_____
_____
_____
_____
_____
_____
_____
_____
_____
_____
_____
_____
_____

A MOM'S BATTLE CRY FOR REST

DAY FOUR ~ THE PARTY

I was missing the party!

It wasn't a planned event. People had dropped by, more followed. I had stretched the dinner we had to feed so many. In between cooking or figuring out what else I could scrounge up, I would go out among the guests and gather plates and utensils to wash (so no one would notice the lack).

But I was missing it!

There were a few people close to the door of the kitchen that I would chat with. They were appreciative of all my efforts, seeing my hard work.

Some people were starting to leave, I was upset......

I had a message for one. Another had offered to lend me dessert plates; at this point, I couldn't just run to the store to buy them.

I'm missing the party.

Does this story sound familiar to you? Maybe not.

With most of the entertaining we do these days, people gather around the kitchen where the meal is being prepared and they can talk to the host(s).

But what if there were a Guest of Honor? Do you remember when Jesus visited Mary and Martha's home? Not only was I missing the "party" AND the Guest of Honor but I was making myself so busy in the process that I......

Was missing someone I had an important message for (I was only talking to those near my small kitchen).

AND

I needed something from someone else that I couldn't find at another time or any place else.

Don't miss YOUR party.....which is your life. We are so *busy* serving, cleaning up everyone's messes, and making sure no one sees a lack within us or our surroundings.

Stop and "smell the roses." Look up at the sky. Notice the trees stretching so tall, reaching up just to touch the hem of the Guest of Honor.

I love Psalm 98. It clearly depicts people and the earth rejoicing over the Lord. We should rejoice, sing praise, clap our hands….now *that's* a party!

Oh, sing to the Lord a new song!
For He has done marvelous things;
His right hand and His holy arm have gained Him the victory.
The Lord has made known His salvation;
His righteousness He has revealed in the sight of the nations.
He has remembered His mercy and His faithfulness to the house of Israel;
All the ends of the earth have seen the salvation of our God.

Shout joyfully to the Lord, all the earth;
Break forth in song, rejoice, and sing praises.
Sing to the Lord with the harp,
With the harp and the sound of a psalm,
With trumpets and the sound of a horn;
Shout joyfully before the Lord, the King.

Let the sea roar, and all its fullness,
The world and those who dwell in it;
Let the rivers clap their hands;
Let the hills be joyful together before the Lord,
For He is coming to judge the earth.
With righteousness He shall judge the world,
And the peoples with equity.

I find it amazing how people can cheer over a football game or band, yet they feel awkward rejoicing over the Lord and His goodness.

Matthew 26:28 reads, "For this is My blood of the new

covenant, which is shed for many for the remission of sins."

Jesus made the ultimate sacrifice for you and me; we were bought at a price. We should shout with joy and celebrate His victory.

Colossians 1:9-14, "For this reason, since the day we heard about you, we have not stopped praying for you. We continually ask God to fill you with the knowledge of his will through all the wisdom and understanding that the Spirit gives, so that you may live a life worthy of the Lord and please him in every way: bearing fruit in every good work, growing in the knowledge of God, being strengthened with all power according to his glorious might so that you may have great endurance and patience, and giving *joyful thanks* to the Father, who has qualified you to share in the inheritance of his holy people in the kingdom of light. *For he has rescued us from the dominion of darkness and brought us into the kingdom of the Son he loves, in whom we have redemption, the forgiveness of sins.*"

The Party:

Busyness

Joyful Praise

~

Help me to be truly present and joyful today, Lord. In Jesus' name I pray, Amen.

A MOM'S BATTLE CRY FOR REST

Rest Stop:

Make a joyful shout to the Lord, all you lands!
Serve the Lord with gladness;
Come before His presence with singing.
Know that the Lord, He is God;
It is He who has made us, and not we ourselves;
We are His people and the sheep of His pasture.

Enter into His gates with thanksgiving,
And into His courts with praise.
Be thankful to Him, and bless His name.
For the Lord is good;
His mercy is everlasting,
And His truth endures to all generations.
Psalm 100

_____
_____
_____
_____
_____
_____
_____
_____
_____
_____
_____
_____
_____
_____
_____
_____
_____

LAURA J. MARSHALL

DAY FIVE ~ THE SWORD

"The kingdom of heaven suffers violence, and the violent take it by force." Matthew 11:12

As a teenager, I had never been in or witnessed a physical fight. As an adult, however, I have been in a fight both physically and spiritually. It's interesting to me even now that the physical fight came not long after I had taken sides in the spiritual battle.

Before that I wasn't much of a threat to the enemy. I had asked Jesus into my heart one day while I was watching the 700 Club when I was a teenager. I followed my own path after that and wasn't really aware of Jesus in my life up until I wanted to have my second child baptized. It was my second marriage, my first son being christened in the Catholic Church. My husband was raised Presbyterian and so we found a church not too far from our home and started attending with the intention of getting our son dedicated.

I mark that time as the start of my journey with Jesus. Before that, the Holy Spirit had whispered into my ear on the occasion and tried to direct my steps; however, I had always called this voice my "intuition". I didn't know about the Holy Spirit or his personal work in my life.

Three months before my physical altercation, I was 20 weeks pregnant and found out our baby didn't have a heartbeat. After this time, I wrapped myself in God's word, seeking Him for comfort and purpose…trying to learn more about Jesus. I was thankful not to have to fight my way into work that fateful day, although the reason for staying home wasn't pleasant. My 4-year-old son was sick. All morning I was praying my youngest wouldn't pick up the germs that had wracked my oldest son's body and send me running for a large bowl from the kitchen.

As my son lay on the couch resting, I cleaned up from giving the baby lunch, quietly trying to pick up dishes and toys. It was warm, but with the rain, there was only one window in the house open, the window behind my sons head on the couch. As I was cleaning a voice kept urging me, *"Close the window."* I silently and continually cast it off, ignoring it. The voice became more insistent, a little louder, almost like a thought that wasn't mine. Finally, I stopped what I was doing, straightened up and out loud, said just as forcefully, "It is raining. There is only one window open in the house and I am not closing it." The voice stopped.

Satisfied, I continued on with my day. Little did I know the enemy's plans that I would have to fight against that night; the battle had God tried to protect me from. For He Himself has said, "I will never leave you nor forsake you" so we may boldly say, "The Lord is my helper, I will not fear; what can man do to me?"

I put the kids to bed at 7:30, settling myself on the couch to watch some television with a silent prayer for a restful night's sleep for my sons. The doors were locked, the house cleaned up. As the night wore on I became restless. I called my husband at work. After saying our goodnights, I started for the bathroom to take a tub. For some reason, this night "something" told me to forego this ritual and read my Bible before going to sleep.

At 10:45, I awoke to a noise. I walked out of my bedroom, glancing into our children's room. All was quiet. As I peered into the living room lit partly by the hallway light hanging overhead, I could make out the back of a man leaning the screen from the open window against the wall. My mind couldn't take in what I was seeing as he turned and faced me. Time seemed to stand still. I said, "What are you doing in my house?" Casually, he walked towards me. Thoughts that something had happened to my husband at work crossed my mind.

The last two feet, he flew at me, grabbing me roughly. I started screaming for help and struggling as he flipped off the light switch and dragged me into the living room. I could hear my children yelling for me. He put his hand over my nose and mouth. I was blacking out. I desperately tried to bite him as I was pushed to the floor. I prayed in my head over and over, "Help me God!" That still small voice again, "*Be Still*." I went

limp and he pulled his hand off my face.
 Gulping in deep breaths of air, I yelled to my children, "Stay in your beds and go to sleep." Silence. The man looked at me saying, "That was smart."

There are moments to fight and there are moments to be still. Exodus 14:13-14 says, Moses answered the people, "Do not be afraid. Stand firm and you will see the deliverance the Lord will bring you today. The Egyptians you see today you will never see again. The Lord will fight for you; you need only to be still."

Jeremiah 1:19 reads: They will fight against you, But they shall not prevail against you. For I am with you," says the Lord, "to deliver you."

The physical fight so well reflects the spiritual fight we have daily with the enemy. While you're trying to rebuild the wall…the connection between yourself and the Lord, care for your family and home, stay healthy, stay strong, the enemy has other plans. Surely, he will try to dissuade you from the idea of getting closer to God, reading His word, praying, and getting the rest you need to be who God has called you to be.

Let's visit Nehemiah 4: But it so happened, when Sanballat heard that we were rebuilding the wall, that he was furious and very indignant, and mocked the Jews. And he spoke before his brethren and the army of Samaria, and said, "What are these feeble Jews doing? Will they fortify themselves? Will they offer sacrifices? Will they complete it in a day? Will they revive the stones from the heaps of rubbish—stones that are burned?"

Now Tobiah the Ammonite was beside him, and he said, "Whatever they build, if even a fox goes up on it, he will break down their stone wall."

I see our enemy in this passage.

Continuing on in verse 6-9, So we built the wall, and the entire wall was joined together up to half its height, for the people had a mind to work. Now it happened, when Sanballat, Tobiah, the Arabs, the Ammonites, and the Ashdodites heard that the walls of Jerusalem were being restored and the gaps were beginning to be closed, that they became very angry, and all of them conspired together to come and attack Jerusalem and create confusion. Nevertheless we made our prayer to our God, and because of them we set a watch against them day and night.

Let's pray and set a watch against the enemy.

Verses 10-11, Then Judah said, "The strength of the laborers is failing, and there is so much rubbish that we are not able to build the wall." And our adversaries said, "They will neither know nor see anything, till we come into their midst and kill them and cause the work to cease."

So much rubbish....busyness, exhaustion, distraction that our strength is failing.

Verses 12-14, So it was, when the Jews who dwelt near

them came, that they told us ten times, "From whatever place you turn, they will be upon us." Therefore I positioned men behind the lower parts of the wall, at the openings; and I set the people according to their families, with their swords, their spears, and their bows. And I looked, and arose and said to the nobles, to the leaders, and to the rest of the people, "Do not be afraid of them. Remember the Lord, great and awesome, and fight for your brethren, your sons, your daughters, your wives, and your houses."

Take your position on the wall with your weapons, fight for your families.

Nehemiah 4:15, And it happened, when our enemies heard that it was known to us, and that God had brought their plot to nothing, that all of us returned to the wall, everyone to his work.

God brought their plot to nothing.

Verses 16-20, So it was, from that time on, that half of my servants worked at construction, while the other half held the spears, the shields, the bows, and wore armor; and the leaders were behind all the house of Judah. Those who built on the wall, and those who carried burdens, loaded themselves so that with one hand they worked at construction, and with the other held a weapon. Every one of the builders had his sword girded at his side as he built. And the one who sounded the trumpet was beside me. Then I said to the nobles, the rulers, and the rest of the people, "The work is great and extensive, and we are separated far from one another on the wall. Wherever you hear the sound of the trumpet, rally to us there. Our God will fight for us."

Yes, Our God will fight for us.

Ephesians 6:10-13, Finally, my brethren, be strong in the Lord and in the power of His might. Put on the whole armor of God, that you may be able to stand against the wiles of the devil. For we do not wrestle against flesh and blood, but against principalities, against powers, against the rulers of the darkness of this age, against spiritual hosts of wickedness in the heavenly places. Therefore take up the whole armor of God, that you may be able to withstand in the evil day, and having done all, to stand.

What are the weapons we have to fight the enemy with?

Verses 14-20, Stand therefore, having girded your waist with truth, having put on the breastplate of righteousness, and having shod your feet with the preparation of the gospel of peace; above all, taking the shield of faith with which you will be able to quench all the fiery darts of the wicked one. And take the helmet of salvation, and the sword of the Spirit, which is the Word of God; praying always with all prayer and supplication in the Spirit, being watchful to this end with all perseverance and supplication for all the saints.

Our weapons are faith, joy, love, our prayers, our relationship with Jesus and putting on Christ, the Word of God, maintaining our ground, the Holy Spirit, truth, sincerity, and a good conscience. These things have substance, real substance in the spiritual world.

1 Thessalonians 5:8, But since we belong to the day, let us be sober, putting on faith and love as a breastplate, and the hope of salvation as a helmet.

2 Thessalonians 3:3, But the Lord is faithful, and he will strengthen you and protect you from the evil one.

1 Thessalonians 5:16-18, Rejoice always, pray continually, give thanks in all circumstances; for this is God's will for you in Christ Jesus.

Nehemiah 8:10 says, The joy of the Lord is your strength.

The Sword:

Battle

Our Weapons

~

Help me to put on my armor today, Lord and be confident that you are with me. In Jesus' name I pray, Amen.

Rest Stop:

The Lord will go forth like a warrior, He will arouse His zeal like a man of war. He will utter a shout, yes, He will raise a war cry. He will prevail against His enemies.
Isaiah 42:13

LAURA J. MARSHALL

DAY SIX ~ THE ROBE

Someday soon a bathrobe may become nonexistent, at least in my house. I can't remember the last time I wore my soft, fluffy, pink bathrobe. I think I would be embarrassed to answer the door in my bathrobe. It almost screams "LAZY" to me. Why is it so shameful to rest, to *need* rest?

A bathrobe should actually yell, "PLANNED REST".

In the Bible, there are quite a few references to "the day of preparation" as in Mark 15:42, "Now when evening had come, because it was the Preparation Day, that is, the day before the Sabbath."

I don't know how I've missed the fact of preparation for rest all of these years. Purposeful planned rest.

Exodus 16:22-23 reads, "And so it was, on the sixth day, that they gathered twice as much bread, two omers for each one. And all the rulers of the congregation came and told Moses. Then he said to them, "This is what the Lord has said: 'Tomorrow is a Sabbath rest, a holy Sabbath to the Lord. Bake what you will bake today, and boil what you will boil; and lay up for yourselves all that remains, to be kept until morning."

In the same way you would prepare for a trip or company coming over, you can and should prepare for your time of rest. There are mental preparations we should make as well as physical. When my children are starting to look like they need a haircut, I start preparing myself and them mentally for the battle of tears and protests. I announce haircut day at least a week in advance, "I'm giving haircuts this weekend, on Saturday afternoon". Preparation and voicing your intent are needed, for you and many times for those around you.

Learning about how the Jewish Days are counted from 6 PM to 6 PM has helped me mentally prepare for a time of planned rest. We mark our days from 12 midnight to 12 midnight. When God created the earth, the Bible reads, "And God called the light Day, and the darkness he called Night. And the evening and the morning were the first day". A Biblical 24 hour day starts in the evening.

If I am planning a time of rest, I will clean up from dinner, help the kids get some of their things settled, and maybe throw in a last load of laundry. One of my most favored planned rests is sitting on the screened in back porch after church on a sunny day and watching the kids play soccer in the backyard (with their older brother and his friends). I inevitably drift off to sleep after writing in my journal and reflecting on the beautiful world around me. The kids run past me about a million times, running for drinks and snacks to share.

I hear their voices at a distance, like comforting voices blurred by the heaviness of contentment. We all need "Sunday Afternoon" moments in our lives.

You may want to plan your rest time while the kids are at school, alone or with friends. Throughout Scripture we see how friends can refresh us, here are two examples:

Acts 27:3, And the next day we touched at Sidon. And Julius courteously entreated Paul, and gave him liberty to go unto his friends to refresh himself.

1 Corinthians 16:17-18, I am glad about the coming of Stephanas, Fortunatus, and Achaicus, for what was lacking on your part they supplied. For they refreshed my spirit and yours. Therefore acknowledge such men.

Of course, this also depends on your choice of friends.

One of the things I have found most helpful has been to cling to the remembrance of my *planned rest* during the week. Life can be touch and go having five sons. There are times in each and every week when I feel overwhelmed, either with housework, feeling my own inadequacies, or fighting little boys and the amount of discipline and being "on watch" that requires.

In 1 Samuel 7, God helped the Israelites subdue the Philistines. In verse 12 the Bible reads, "Then Samuel took a stone and set it up between Mizpah and Shen. He named it Ebenezer, saying, "Thus far the Lord has helped us." Ebenezer means "stone of help".

In the Scriptures, the Israelites created stone memorials. Stones of remembrance. I incorporate these "stones" into my own life. When I have experienced *planned rest*, I have "stones of remembrance" to look back on even in my toughest moments. I remember what I did or didn't do, and the refreshment that came from that time. I gain strength and perspective in the reflection. I praise God for His goodness of incorporating rest into my life. In my busyness, I would tend to keep going and forget, but He draws me back and reminds me of the importance of resting from my work.

The Robe:

Preparation

Memorials

~

Dear Lord, Help me to plan some rest for my body into my week. In Jesus' name I pray, Amen.

Rest Stop:

Then the apostles gathered to Jesus and told Him all things, both what they had done and what they had taught. And He said to them, "Come aside by yourselves to a deserted place and rest a while." For there were many coming and going, and they did not even have time to eat. So they departed to a deserted place in the boat by themselves.
Mark 6:30-32

DAY SEVEN ~ THE TUB

Anyone who colors their hair knows that you don't take a tub when you're coloring your hair. If you washed out the color in the tub, you would be covered in dye from your head to your toes.

Today with a piece of chocolate in one hand and hair color fermenting atop my silvery roots, I sought out my tub. Where do you find your physical rest? Would it look foolish to the world?

We are more than our physical selves, yet to deny that part or to listen to it wholly will never give us rest. Remember how I rested for days on end when I wasn't well, resting physically yet unable to *feel* rested?

"Come to Me, all you who labor and are heavy laden, and I will give you rest." Jesus' words. Just to read them again gives my soul a longing and sweet pause.

Here is the entire Scripture in Matthew 11:28-30, "Come to Me, all you who labor and are heavy laden, and I will give you rest. Take My yoke upon you and learn from Me, for I am gentle and lowly in heart, and you will find rest for your souls. For My yoke is easy and My burden is light."

In the past, these words have caused me to clamor. Clamor for His attention and to achieve this seemingly unattainable thing…rest for the weary.

I am weary. I have been weary. In the future, I may become weary. I am grateful for the guidance God has given me in His Word on how to come to Jesus. How do I come to you, Jesus?

Matthew 18:2-5, Then Jesus called a little child to Him, set him in the midst of them, and said, "Assuredly, I say to you, unless you are converted and become as little children, you will by no means enter the kingdom of heaven. Therefore whoever humbles himself as this little child is the greatest in the kingdom of heaven. Whoever receives one little child like this in My name receives Me."

I didn't ask about being great in the kingdom of heaven, but how to come to you, Jesus.

Yes, but you must come like a child…who willingly comes when beckoned, who trusts and easily responds to love.

Faith. We must know and believe Jesus is who He says He is and He will whisk away the world to lean close and hear our whispered words, the unspoken aches of our heart, and that He is merciful and loving and will help us.

Let's visit Matthew 20:29-34:

As Jesus and his disciples were leaving Jericho, a large crowd followed him. Two blind men were sitting by the roadside, and when they heard that Jesus was going by, they shouted, "Lord, Son of David, have mercy on us!"

They knew who Jesus was and called out to Him.

The crowd rebuked them and told them to be quiet, but they shouted all the louder, "Lord, Son of David, have mercy on us!"

The two blind men ignored the world and kept shouting.

Jesus stopped and called them. "What do you want me to do for you?" he asked.

Jesus focused on their cries and stopped to listen. He asked what He could do for them.

"Lord," they answered, "we want our sight."

They believed Jesus could heal them.

Jesus had compassion on them and touched their eyes. Immediately they received their sight and followed Him.

The Greek word for compassion is splagchnon. Strong's Concordance defines it as "the inward parts; the heart, affections, seat of the feelings." Their belief, actions, and words touched the heart of our Lord and He reached out to touch and heal them.

I believe Jesus wants us to reach our full potential in Him. He wants to help us in every little thing. If "little foxes spoil the vine" then wouldn't it be wise to go to Jesus with even our littlest worries and needs? It may seem like a little thing, a time of rest, but it can make or break a marriage, a mother, a household, a job.

Do we really *need* to rest though, physically, and be consciously aware of the moments we carve out? Is it that important?

According to God's word, yes it is. We are not under the law anymore, but under grace. However, in Exodus 23:12 (KJV), the Bible says, "Six days you shall do your work, and on the seventh day you shall rest, that your ox and your donkey may rest, and the son of your female servant and the stranger may be *refreshed*."

Don't you want to feel refreshed? I do! Sab'-ath (shabbath, shabbathon; sabbaton, ta sabbata) the root shabhath in Hebrew means "to desist," "cease," "rest".

I've heard the Sabbath described as, when we are in Christ, our salvation, our life, our eternity. We have entered into the finished work of Christ and have ceased from our own works and are *living* in the Sabbath.

Colossians 2:10 says, "For he who has entered His rest has himself also ceased from his works as God did from

His."

It is so easy that it's hard to understand and achieve. I continually come to the Lord. I continually confess my weakness, in my flesh and of my mind to *rest in my salvation*, my Sabbath.

The world has forgotten how to rest and the church has shamed us into making "a Sabbath" a thing that we fight over in our Christian circles.

The soul finds rest in Jesus and the body needs rest from work. Our Mommy brains in this beautiful broken world need rest from our anxious thoughts. Did you know that even the land rests?

Zachariah 1:10-11 reads:

And the man who stood among the myrtle trees answered and said, "These are the ones whom the Lord has sent to walk to and fro throughout the earth." So they answered the Angel of the Lord, who stood among the myrtle trees, and said, "We have walked to and fro throughout the earth, and behold, *all the earth is resting quietly.*"

Leviticus 25:1-4 reads:

And the Lord spoke to Moses on Mount Sinai, saying, "Speak to the children of Israel, and say to them: 'When you come into the land which I give you, then *the land shall keep a sabbath to the Lord.* Six years you shall sow your field, and six years you shall prune your vineyard, and gather its fruit; but in the seventh year there shall be a Sabbath of *solemn rest for the land*, a Sabbath to the Lord. You shall neither sow your field nor prune your vineyard."

The tub allows my body to rest physically yet my mind and soul ponder and rest on the Lord's finished work. I reflect as the hot water pours from the spout and masks the busy house sounds of little boys' laughter or tears, barking dogs, and voices from near and far. The Lord is the oasis for my soul and when I physically cultivate moments of planned rest, it's like a beautiful garden has blossomed and gives fragrance to myself, those around me, and God above.

Hosea 14:7

Those who dwell under his shadow shall return;
They shall be *revived* like grain,
And grow like a vine.
Their scent shall be like the wine of Lebanon.

The Tub:

Rest

~

Lord, Give me wisdom and help me to rest. In Jesus' name I pray, Amen.

A Mom's Battle Cry for Rest

Rest Stop:

Catch us the foxes,
The little foxes that spoil the vines,
For our vines have tender grapes.
Song of Solomon 2:15

LAURA J. MARSHALL

IN THE END

The piles don't yell at me anymore. I don't know exactly where along this journey they became silent and I took back authority over my time. I have let God's voice be louder as I read His word, stay close to Him in prayer, and put my days in His hands.

For some this will be a hard teaching. There is so much strife, just as in the days of the Pharisees, over doctrine and dividing the Word. I come to the Lord as a child. He loves me. When I ask for wisdom, He fills me with just enough not to overwhelm me. The way I approach rest has worked for me. If I skip a week, two weeks, a month of having a planned time of rest then I can tell and so can others in my life, although they don't understand why I am less patient and more flustered. Try it. I believe you will be pleasantly surprised at the abundance of refreshment.

I love the Lord. He loves me back. Oh, how He loves me back. From the moment God had a thought of me, He loved me. Despite sin and selfishness, in my acts of filthy righteousness, He loves me.

Throughout this book, I've made an assumption: That

you know Jesus Christ as your Lord and Savior.

Jesus is the easiest initial decision I've ever made. However, I decide every day, every moment who I will serve. It's not easy. It's the hardest *life* decision I have ever made. If today you hear His voice, do not harden your heart.

Jesus longs to be your Savior, your Warrior, your Husband, your Well.

The keys are repentance. Acts 2:38, Then Peter said to them, "Repent, and let every one of you be baptized in the name of Jesus Christ for the remission of sins; and you shall receive the gift of the Holy Spirit."

And belief…faith in Jesus. Acts 16:29-32 reads, Then he called for a light, ran in, and fell down trembling before Paul and Silas. And he brought them out and said, "Sirs, what must I do to be saved?" So they said, "Believe on the Lord Jesus Christ, and you will be saved, you and your household." Then they spoke the word of the Lord to him and to all who were in his house.

Romans 10:5-13, For Moses writes about the righteousness which is of the law, "The man who does those things shall live by them." But the righteousness of faith speaks in this way, "Do not say in your heart, 'Who will ascend into heaven?'" (that is, to bring Christ down from above) or, "'Who will descend into the abyss?'" (that is, to bring Christ up from the dead). But what does it say? "The word is near you, in your mouth and in your heart" (that is, the word of faith which we preach): that if you confess with your mouth the Lord Jesus and believe in your heart that God has raised Him from the dead, you will be saved. For with the heart one believes unto righteousness, and with the mouth confession is made unto salvation. For the Scripture says, "Whoever believes on Him will not be put to shame." For there is no distinction between Jew and Greek, for the same Lord over all is rich to all who call upon Him. For "whoever calls on the name of the Lord shall be saved."

In the end…..Jesus answered and said to her, "Martha, Martha, you are worried and troubled about many things. But one thing is needed, and Mary has chosen that *good part*, which will not be taken away from her."

Rest Stop:

The Lord your God in your midst,
The Mighty One, will save;
He will rejoice over you with gladness,
He will quiet you with His love,
He will rejoice over you with singing.
Zephaniah 3:17

A NOTE AND GIFT FROM LAURA

If you liked this book, please stop in and leave a review online at one of the major book retailers so that other moms can hear what you think about the book.

As a gift for reading the first book in the Battle Cry Devotional series, I'd like to offer you a bookplate for your paperback copy of *A Mom's Battle Cry for Rest*. These are limited in number, so check my website for availability under the books link at the top of the page.

ABOUT THE AUTHOR

Laura J. Marshall lives in Virginia. She writes fiction and nonfiction. You can find out more about Laura and her other books online on her website at www.LauraJMarshall.com. *A Mom's Battle Cry to Overcome Fear* (excerpt enclosed) and *A Mom's Battle Cry for Health & Beauty* will be releasing in 2013 along with her Fiction novella, *Persistent Love*.

A Mom's Battle Cry for Rest

LAURA J. MARSHALL

A MOM'S BATTLE CRY FOR REST

Excerpt from *A Mom's Battle Cry to Overcome Fear* by Laura J. Marshall

When God first brought this book to mind as I wrote the chapter "The Sword" in *A Mom's Battle Cry for Rest*, I resisted the thought. Later, as again it was brought before me, I cried out in my head, "I can't!" That's when I knew that somewhere deep down fear still had me in it's grip and though it wasn't somewhere I lived, a part of me was still enslaved.

Several nights later, I had dreams of running through a large home, locking the many windows and doors. They didn't seem secure enough or strong enough to keep whatever it was I was afraid of out. It was there. It lurked and watched me. I could see one door was still open, yet it was unreachable. The dogs outside in the yard barked and pawed the ground. They felt the watching too. Did they sense my fear? I cried deep inside, "I don't want to live there again."

But here I am again; I take this journey with you. Not from the same depths as before, but I climb again and make the ascent.

This is a Mom's Battle Cry to Overcome Fear.

LAURA J. MARSHALL

A MOM'S BATTLE CRY FOR REST

Made in the USA
Charleston, SC
19 February 2013